Band of Beavers - Kick it! / First published: December 2021
Facebook page: "Band of Beavers"

Dedicated to my wife and boys. You are my everything. (Chuck)
Thank you Kirsten. And Joanie, your skill is amazing!

To my partner, family and friends; thank you for always encouraging me
to follow my dreams. (Joanie)

BOOOOOOOOOOM!

A bunch of beavers loved to play.
All day and every day.
Friends since they were small.
Soccer, their game, or as some
say... football.

Kickaround Beavers you say?
That's impossible! There is no
way!
Beavers are meant for hockey,
that's their game.
Ice, snow and hockey pucks, their
claim to fame.

Beavers playing soccer? What?

Other animals would snicker.
"No Beaver is meant to be a
kicker!"
But our team replied, "play we
shall!
This game gives us high morale.

Kick, pass and shoot.
Is such a hoot.
In unison, we'll have each others'
back.
As one, we are a pack.

Look at this!

"Nothing will distract us.
We will practice and practice.
A common goal to be the best we
can.
We'll show this forest, our able
brand."

Suddenly a golden shot came
about.
They'd enter a tournament
without a doubt.
Beavers and the beautiful game
are not bizarre.
They'll show the world how good
they are.

Look at those silly beavers!

Others continued to laugh and
joke.
"You'll be smashed, blown out or
smoked!
No chance, you have! Beavers
can't compete.
Stop this silly dream, you only
have left feet!"

The beavers faced, with a choice
to make.
Give it all up, or eat the cake?
Be brave and take the challenge
head on.
The Band of Beavers took up the
baton.

Far from home.

Ready to prove to the planet.
United! They are strong as
granite.
Packed with speed, skill and
smarts.
They are built on hungry hearts.

They arrived in a land far from
home.
Eager, but nervous the thoughts in
their dome.
Against lions and tigers or bears -
oh my!
These battles may produce a black
eye.

Head-to-head!

The journey of twists and turns
had begun.
The host Arabian Oryx, in Game
number 1.
Our heroes' strategy they decided
to apply.
A defensive fortress - which
earned them a tie. (0-0)

Not beaten to shreds. They turned
some heads.
"Better than expected", is what
someone said.
But they'll need to score and not
simply hold fort.
As tickling the twine is the nature
of sport!

Beavers vs Rufous Hornero (skilled birds).

Up next, the crafty Rufous Horneros.
Our squad played on the straight and narrow.
They worked hard and did as they could.
And a late lucky goal, our warriors had withstood.
(Tie - 1-1).

Hey, not too bad! Two ties, in two matches.
Bumps, bruises and a few nasty scratches.
If by a miracle, our heroes did win…
A playoff spot! And a celebration would begin.

GOOOOOOOOOOOOOOOOOAL!!!

Due to the outcomes the team
had achieved.
Friends from home started to
believe.
"Maybe those beavers were right
all along?
Together, they truly are strong!"

Forthcoming the bulldogs from an
island nation.
"Their dream will be over", was
others' summation.
But with a powerful WHACK - of a
Beaver tail slap.
They had won! And we're now on
the map! (WIN 1-0)

We won't be intimidated by any Eagle!

The mighty Gallic Roosters, up
next for a fight.
This fairytale seemed to have no
end in sight.
Low and behold, with a kiss off
the post!
A victory sealed on a goal scored
coast to coast.
WIN 2-1

Then the Eagles swoop in with
their skill.
Their barrage of attacks fended
off. What a thrill!
Our goalie stood tall facing
kick-after-kick.
A penalty shootout win, on a slick
tail flick!
WIN (penalties 1-0)

Un-BEAVER-lievable!

The Grey Wolves expected an
easy beaver meal.
But could this be happening,
could this be real?
A legendary story told for years to
come.
The kids' win again and leave their
foe numb.
WIN 2-0

At home, the forest dwellers all
cheer.
As the final match drew near.
Chants from the North, South,
East and West!
"Our brave beavers are the best."

This is it! Let's do this!

Our heroes fight the lions all
night.
With a championship trophy in
sight.
But as the final whistle blew.
They had sadly lost 3 to 2.

After suffering this crushing
defeat.
The experience now feels
bittersweet.
So close to the prize.
There are a few tears in their eyes.

Return of our CHAMPS!

But they take a moment to think.
"We should be proud! We went to
the brink."
Beavers banding together, is such
a treat.
And can accomplish any
astonishing feat!

Once home they receive a
thunderous reception.
And cement the new forest
perception.
"Believer Beavers are real", with
cheers all around.
You are the heroes of our
hometown."